ROSALIND LOOKED CLOSER

An Unsung Hero of Molecular Science

by **Lisa Gerin**

illustrated by
Chiara Fedele

beaming books
MINNEAPOLIS

28 27 26 25 24 23 22   1 2 3 4 5 6 7 8 9

Hardcover ISBN: 978-1-5064-7065-8
eBook ISBN: 978-1-5064-7066-5

Photo of Rosalind Franklin: © agefotostock 2022; Rosalind Franklin (1920–1958), British chemist. Pioneer molecular biologist by the *Jewish Chronicle*.

Special thanks to Dr. Nicholas Reiter and Dr. Martin St. Maurice from Marquette University for consulting on this book.

Library of Congress Cataloging-in-Publication Data

Names: Gerin, Lisa, author. | Fedele, Chiara, illustrator.
Title: Rosalind looked closer : the unsung hero of molecular science / by
  Lisa Gerin ; illustrated by Chiara Fedele.
Description: Minneapolis : Beaming Books, 2022. | Includes bibliographical
  references. | Audience: Ages 5-8 | Summary: "A picture book biography
  about scientist Rosalind Franklin and her contributions to molecular
  biology, discovery of the DNA double helix, and study of viruses"--
  Provided by publisher.
Identifiers: LCCN 2021047682 (print) | LCCN 2021047683 (ebook) | ISBN
  9781506470658 (hardcover) | ISBN 9781506470665 (ebook)
Subjects: LCSH: Franklin, Rosalind, 1920-1958--Juvenile literature. | Women
  molecular biologists--Great Britain--Biography--Juvenile literature. |
  DNA--History--Juvenile literature.
Classification: LCC QH506 .G46 2022 (print) | LCC QH506 (ebook) | DDC
  572.8/092 [B]--dc23/eng/20211028
LC record available at https://lccn.loc.gov/2021047682
LC ebook record available at https://lccn.loc.gov/2021047683

VN0004589; 9781506470658; JUN2022

Beaming Books
PO Box 1209
Minneapolis, MN 55440-1209
Beamingbooks.com

"Science and everyday life cannot and should not be separated."

—Rosalind Franklin

To my daughters, Halli and Marissa, with love.
—LG

To my daughter Margherita.
And all the brave girls around the world.
—CF

Eight-year-old Rosalind loved playing in Kensington Gardens with her brothers. She hunted for butterflies and collected interesting plants. Then she brought them inside to look closer at them with her microscope.

Most people in 1920s London didn't think girls should do those things. Girls were supposed to wear pretty dresses or plant flowers.

"When I grow up, I want to become a scientist," Rosalind said.

"Girls can't be scientists," her father told her.

"Girls can do anything," her mother said.

When Rosalind was nine, her parents
sent her away to boarding school.
She was the only Jewish girl there.
While the other girls attended church, Rosalind studied Hebrew
with a private teacher. She studied Latin, French, and German too.

She loved taking long walks near mountains and snapping photos of their purple peaks surrounded by wispy clouds.

At age eleven, she returned home and went to one of the few schools in London that taught science to girls, St. Paul's Girls School.

Rosalind mixed and measured as she studied chemistry. She poured bright blue liquids into glass beakers. She computed difficult math problems, balanced equations, and *never* gave up until she had the solution. *Rosalind always took a closer look*.

Soon the threat of World War II loomed over Rosalind's life. While she swirled and separated chemicals in the lab at school, violence and hatred were dividing the world. It was the late 1930s. The powerful leader of the Nazi Party, Adolf Hitler, forced Jewish families in Germany and surrounding countries to leave their homes. Shopkeepers' windows were smashed. Families were divided. A lot of people were hurt and even killed. Many Jewish people fled to safer countries.

Rosalind and her four siblings realized how lucky they were living in England where Jewish people were protected.

When Rosalind graduated high school, she received a full
scholarship to Cambridge University to study chemistry.
There she examined different types of coals and carbons under
a microscope. She wanted to see which ones were safe to use
in gas masks worn by soldiers. Rosalind's research helped the
British government make safer gas masks for soldiers.

Rosalind's father still didn't think women should be scientists. He wanted her to help others by becoming a social worker, or working for the government, or raising a family.

She wrote him many letters from college.

Dear Father:

You look at science as some sort of invention of man,
something apart from real life.
But science and everyday life
cannot and should not be separated.

Rosalind

The war ended and Rosalind graduated from the university. She moved to Paris where she had a job as a research chemist in a government lab. Rosalind studied how different carbons reacted to heat.

She learned a new scientific technique called X-ray diffraction. This was a way to learn about the atomic structure of molecules in three-dimensional space. Looking through a microscope, Rosalind saw a fairytale world of clustered molecules that looked like tiny snowflakes. She focused the X-ray beam and photographed how her X-ray beam was scattered by the symmetrical molecules in the sample. The unique pattern she observed told her about the shape and structure of the molecule. She worked hard and quickly became the expert in photographing such amazing images.

Rosalind always took a closer look.

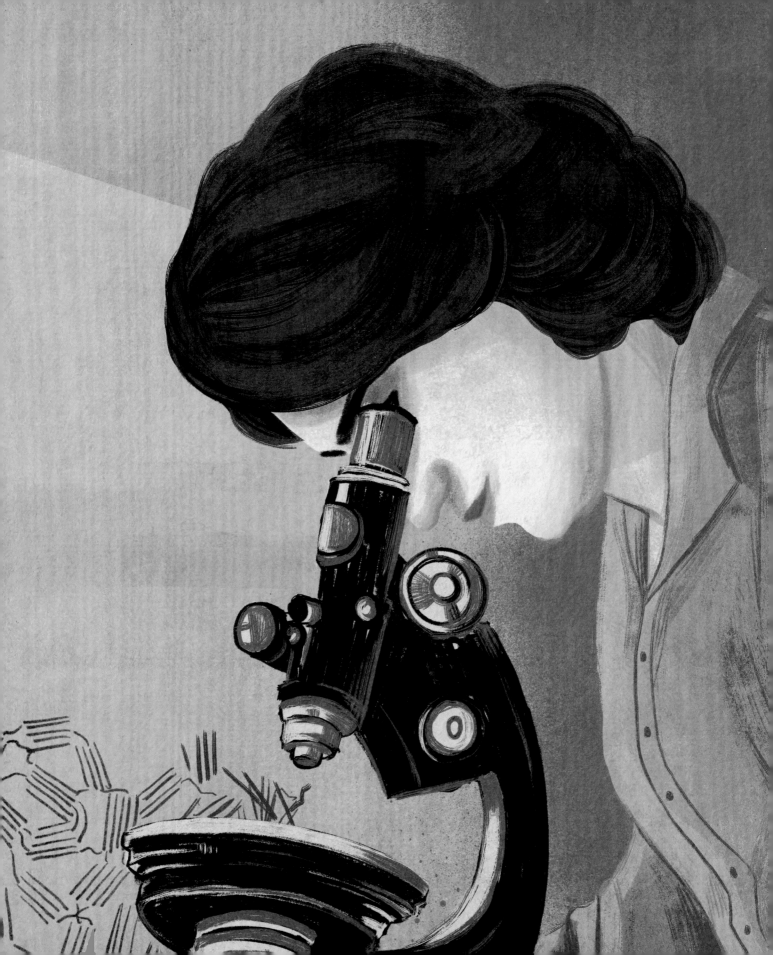

Rosalind left Paris and went back to London to work at a lab at Kings College.

Rosalind and her lab partner, Maurice Wilkins, studied the structure of DNA. DNA, or deoxyribonucleic acid, carries the blueprint instructions for life and determines how people or even plants will look or act.

They took *hundreds* of pictures of the DNA molecule.

Other scientists (mostly men) were working on the same thing in Europe and America. Everyone was trying to solve the puzzle of what DNA actually looked like.

After two years, Rosalind got the perfect picture of DNA. It was labeled Photo 51, the fifty-first X-ray picture her lab had taken. Rosalind took a closer look at the photo. She saw an image of a helix made up of repeating strands of DNA. It was mesmerizing. This was what the DNA double helix model looked like up close.

It was unlike any other image that had been seen before. Rosalind's heart soared.

Maurice Wilkins showed the DNA picture to two other scientists. He didn't ask Rosalind's permission. The scientists, James Watson and Francis Crick, realized that Rosalind had captured the best photo of DNA yet, suggesting it was two-sided, not triple-sided.

They wrote an article about their model based partially on Photo 51 and sent it to *Nature*, a scientific journal, without including Rosalind as an author or mentioning her photograph.

Rosalind was a patient scientist. She wrote up her findings, but by the time she was finished, Watson and Crick had already presented their model of DNA based on her data. Rosalind got the very first data showing the structure of DNA but did not receive the credit. The world refused to recognize that a woman had made this discovery.

Rosalind was frustrated, but she refused to give up on science.

The next year, Rosalind began research on viruses. It was the early 1950s and the polio virus was spreading worldwide. A lot of people were getting sick. Scientists were experimenting with finding a vaccine for the disease as quickly as they could. Rosalind got live polio virus samples and kept them in her parents' refrigerator before bringing them to her lab!

Viruses can be composed of RNA, or ribonucleic acid, and protein. RNA is a molecule that is like DNA's cousin. Rosalind knew from studying DNA that a virus could take over healthy cells and produce infections. Who better than she to photograph viruses using X-rays?

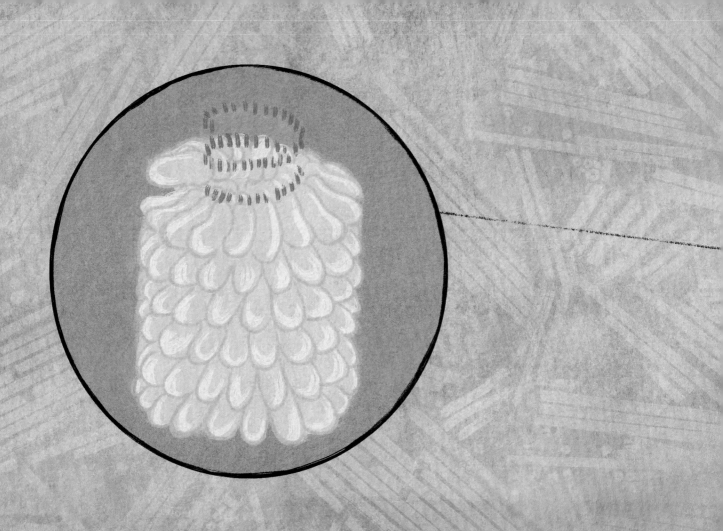

She noticed that RNA in plant viruses was similar in structure to RNA in human viruses. She took pictures of viruses in tobacco mosaic and turnip plants. Just as she was able to show the shape of DNA, now she would show the world the structure of a virus. Her photos showed plant viruses to be cylindrical in shape, with proteins on the outside and RNA threads winding around the inside. Once a virus got inside a healthy host cell, the virus injected its RNA and then the virus took over.

Rosalind always took a closer look.

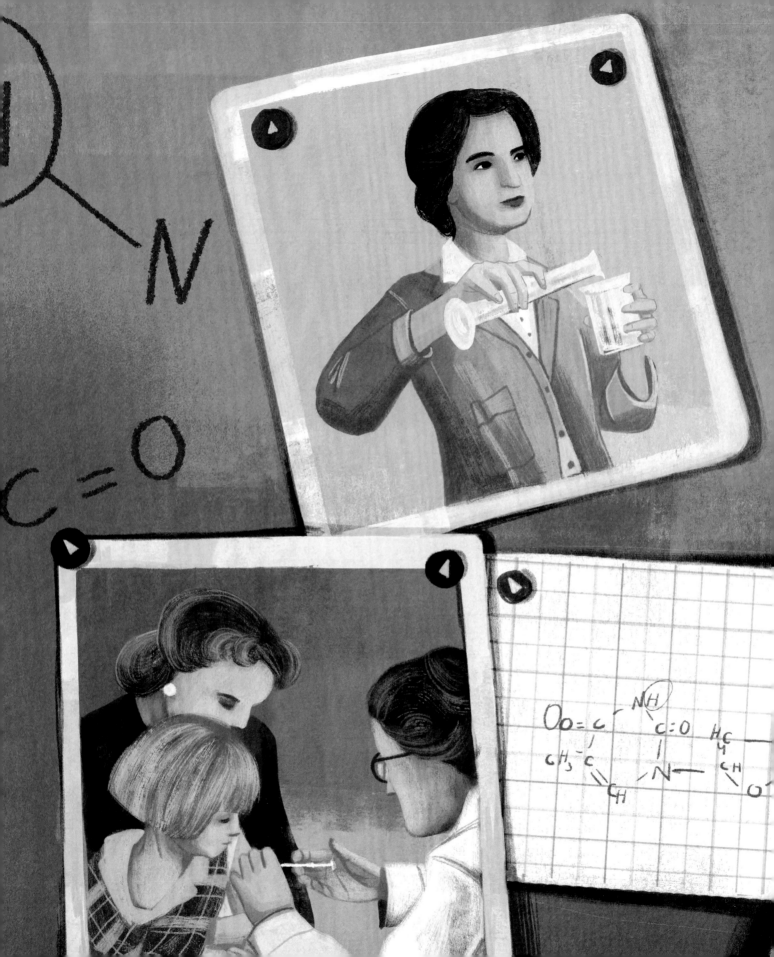

Rosalind spent many years studying plant viruses. She wrote fifteen papers about them. Although the polio vaccine was developed by Dr. Jonas Salk in 1952, there were still many people with the disease.

Rosalind and her colleague researched the shape of polio virus crystals in more detail to help doctors. Because of her research and the vaccine, we know more about the shape of viruses, and children and adults are safe from polio.

News

Salk Polio Vaccine
Safe and Effective

Rosalind was proud to be part of solving problems and helping others. She was the scientist she had dreamed of becoming as a young girl.

Rosalind peered into her microscope and continued to take a closer look.

Author's Note

Rosalind Franklin

Sadly, Rosalind fell ill and died of ovarian cancer when she was only thirty-seven years old. Watson, Crick, and Wilkins received the Nobel Prize for Medicine in 1962. But without Franklin's landmark Photo 51, they would not have made their calculations for the DNA molecule being a double helix. Her colleague Aaron Klug received the Nobel Prize in Chemistry in 1982 for his work on virus research and dedicated it to Rosalind. He said, "Had her life not been cut tragically short, she might well have stood in this place on an earlier occasion."

In 2000, Kings College, London, opened the Franklin-Wilkins Building in her memory, and the Chicago Medical School was renamed the Rosalind Franklin University of Medicine and Science in 2004 in her honor. A beautiful statue of Rosalind stands in the campus square.

In 2019, a new virus began to spread. A novel coronavirus caused a dangerous disease scientists called COVID-19. People all around the world got very sick and many died. Scientists scrambled to learn about this virus and find a way to stop it. They used research methods that Rosalind pioneered through her knowledge of DNA, RNA, and viruses.

In record time, scientists made a new kind of vaccine using messenger RNA to teach bodies to fight the coronavirus. Millions of lives were saved.

Now, people are taking a closer look at Rosalind and thanking her for her groundbreaking scientific work.

Glossary

Diffraction

X-ray diffraction is a way to learn about the structure of a molecule by using X-rays shone through a crystal. A pattern is created that gives a scientist the ability to make a three-dimensional picture of a molecule that wouldn't otherwise be visible. One kind of diffraction is called crystallography.

DNA

DNA is a kind of nucleic acid found in your cells. It holds the information for making new cells and it determines the traits of living things. For example, DNA decides your eye color and your height. It is made up of repeating strands that look like a twisted ladder. DNA is short for "deoxyribonucleic acid."

Microscope

A microscope is an instrument with one or more lenses used to help a person to see something very small by making it appear larger. Scientists use microscopes to look at things too small for the human eye to see by itself.

Polio

Polio is a life-threatening disease caused by a virus. It was once one of the most feared diseases in the United States, but the creation of a vaccine in the 1950s ended the threat. The US is now polio free, though travelers can still bring it into this country. Polio is short for "poliomyelitis."

RNA

RNA is a kind of nucleic acid found in your cells. Unlike DNA, it looks like a single strand instead of a double helix. It leaves the center of the cell to tell the rest of the cell what to do, based on the information from the DNA. RNA also carries genetic information in certain viruses. RNA is short for "ribonucleic acid."

Vaccine

A vaccine is a way to create protection from some diseases. Vaccines teach your immune system how to recognize and fight against harmful germs and viruses.

Virus

A virus causes illness and disease in people, animals, plants, and even bacteria. A virus can multiply in the cells of living things.

Timeline

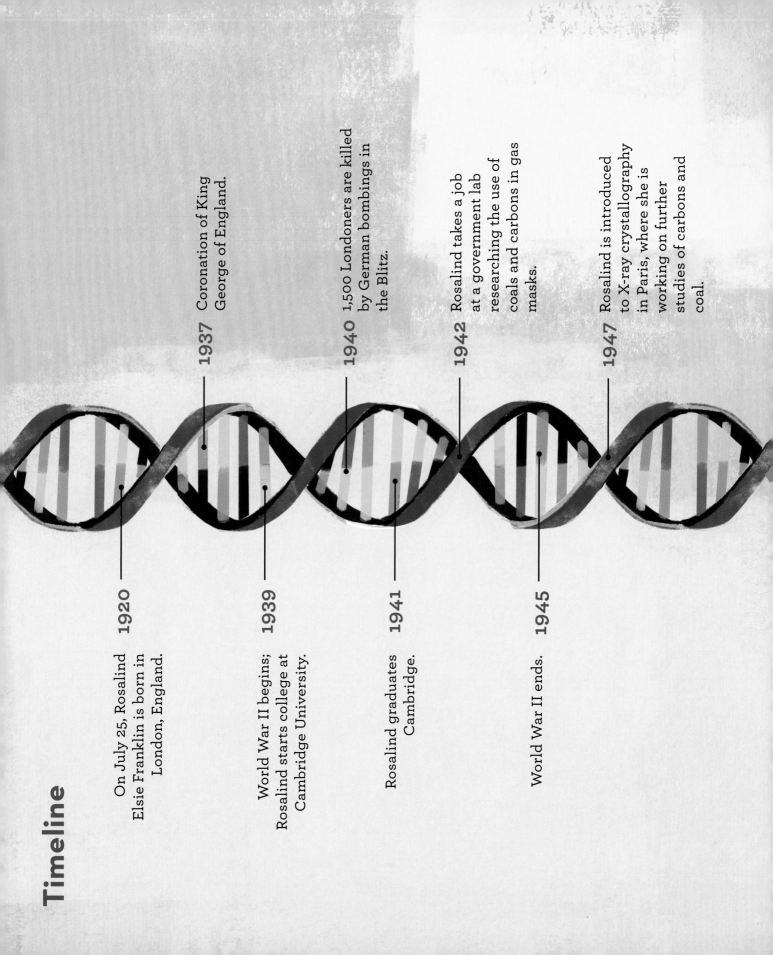

1920
On July 25, Rosalind Elsie Franklin is born in London, England.

1937
Coronation of King George of England.

1939
World War II begins; Rosalind starts college at Cambridge University.

1940
1,500 Londoners are killed by German bombings in the Blitz.

1941
Rosalind graduates Cambridge.

1942
Rosalind takes a job at a government lab researching the use of coals and carbons in gas masks.

1945
World War II ends.

1947
Rosalind is introduced to X-ray crystallography in Paris, where she is working on further studies of carbons and coal.

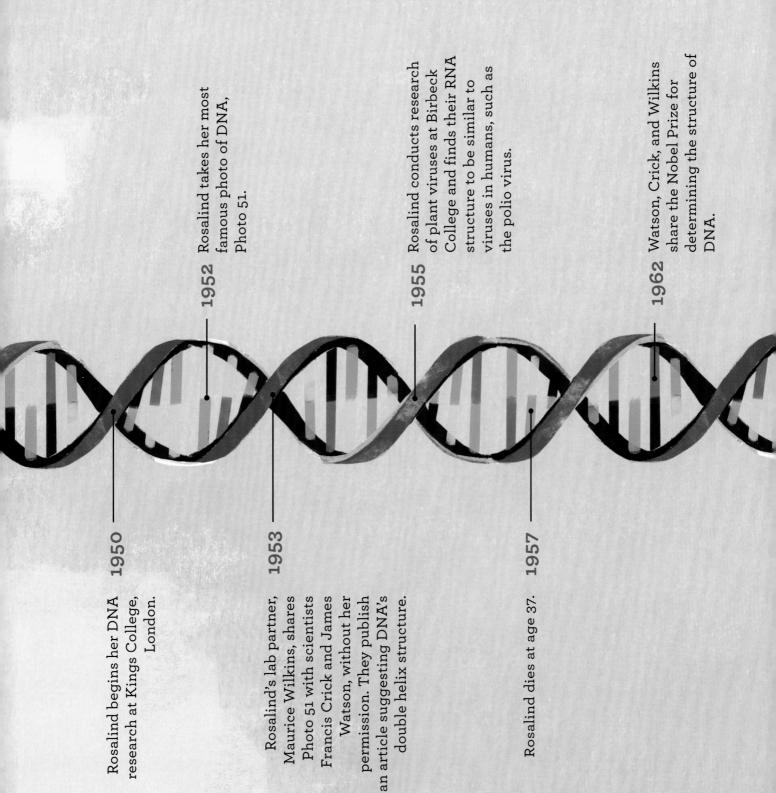

1950 Rosalind begins her DNA research at Kings College, London.

1952 Rosalind takes her most famous photo of DNA, Photo 51.

1953 Rosalind's lab partner, Maurice Wilkins, shares Photo 51 with scientists Francis Crick and James Watson, without her permission. They publish an article suggesting DNA's double helix structure.

1955 Rosalind conducts research of plant viruses at Birbeck College and finds their RNA structure to be similar to viruses in humans, such as the polio virus.

Rosalind dies at age 37. **1957**

1962 Watson, Crick, and Wilkins share the Nobel Prize for determining the structure of DNA.

Select Bibliography

Elkin, Lynne. "Rosalind Elsie Franklin." In *Jewish Women: A Comprehensive Historical Encyclopedia.* Jewish Women's Archive, December 31, 1999. https://jwa.org/encyclopedia/article/franklin-rosalind.

Johnson, Ben. "Rosalind Franklin's Contributions to Virology." *Springer Nature* 25 (July 2017). https://naturemicrobiologycommunity.nature.com/posts/18900-rosalind-franklin-s-contributions-to-virology.

Maddox, Brenda. *Rosalind Franklin: The Dark Lady of DNA.* New York: Harper Collins, 2002.

"Rosalind Franklin and the Most Important Photo Ever Taken." Science Museum of Virginia, April 23, 2021, https://smv.org/learn/blog/rosalind-franklin-and-most-important-photo-ever-taken/

Sayre, Anne. *Rosalind Franklin and DNA.* New York: Norton, 1975.

Watson, James D. *The Double Helix: A Personal Account of the Discovery of the Structure of DNA.* Critical ed. Edited by Gunther Stent. New York: Norton, 1980. (Original edition published in 1968.)

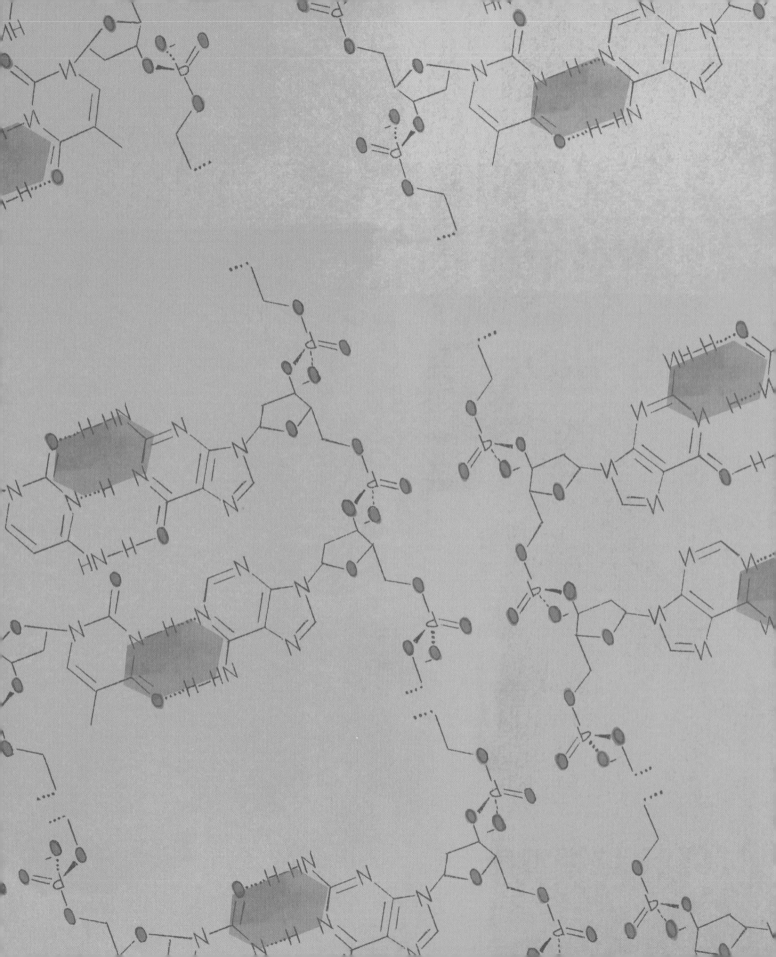